Inverse

Inverse

informed
thoughts by an
unfit poet

Holly
Brians Ragusa

Amused Moon

For the world of words lost
to cruelty, conformity and superiority

Inverse; informed thoughts by an unfit poet
Copyright © 2023 by Holly Brians Ragusa
Amused Moon February 2023

LCCN 2023900452
Subject: Poetry

Printed in the United States of America on acid-free paper

ACKNOWLEDGEMENTS

- "She is the Shield She Wears" -Published anthology *She Speaks Up!* -selected National Jessie Butler Poetry Contest June 2020.
- "True Grime"- Published Willowdown Books Nature Anthology February 14, 2020
- "In the Stew"- Published The Well Mindful Poetry April 29, 2020
- "Gyre"- Published Earth Journal October 2021
- "Two Candles"- Published Common Threads, Ohio Poetry Association Fall 2021
- "Graveyard"- Published SOS Art For a Better World May 2021
- "Wright From Wrong" inspired by Richard Wright Haiku (Arcade Publishing, 1998)

Photography credit Holly Brians Ragusa

- Cover art- Pigeon Parliament on Serpentine Wall Cincinnati Ohio October 2020
- Paris Carrier Pigeon Sculpture in 3rd Arrondissement Paris November 2021
- Omnipotent Paris Raven Jardin du Luxembourg France December 2021
- Protest Vagina Vote poster Cincinnati OH protest march July 2022
- Hemlock Coffee cup reflections Woodward PA October 2021
- Sunflower Shadow Over-the-Rhine Cincinnati OH August 2022
- Ohio River Breaks at Dawn Cincinnati Ohio September 2020

CONTENTS

CONTENTS

CONTENTS

CONTENTS

May these 44 degrees of me, us, she, we
contain contents amply flammable
to alight worthy fires
and warm cold
hearts

Headless in Paris

The pigeon's head was very apparently not present.

Ripped off it seemed. By whom or what I hadn't a clue.

Following the lead of two Parisians just in front of me, I stepped widely around the unknown travesty prior to knowing why. An exclamation crossing language barriers emanated from one of the pedestrians, and as it registered in these ears, these eyes involuntarily glanced down to where other disgusted eyes were already cast. Slightly stained white and black feathers lay oily and squandered beneath the red pucker of the place where a head once was. My lips pursed in disfavor of the scene. Headless in Paris the poor thing. My own turned on a swivel, keeping along on my path, glancing slowly back to better surmise the scene I'd witnessed.

My thoughts returned to the unfortunate pigeon throughout the remainder of my walk, and multiple stories of how it had befallen its end manufactured in my writer's mind.

For how could just such a bird beheading have occurred?

Had it simply charged a window so forcibly that a brain injury swelled and exploded the wee head popping it clean off? Unlikely, yet if so, where was that detached and bloody, beaked ball? Had it rolled away or been collected? Perhaps inadvertently a tourist or local kicked the token tête down the curb. Had a brazen and timely rat seized upon a delicacy? Who knew? Up against the building as it were, prone to its end, only a carcass of incapable wings lay visible on the sidewalk, nothing more.

Natural cause of death likely meant a fall from a ledge after a long life or a rather stiff breeze careening the poor bird at just the right velocity to catch a rough edge on the decorative facade, perfectly severing neck from skull on the six stories down. Possible, as in the realm of all things are, though I've not oft seen a grown bird lose its footing.

Perhaps, my mind, prone to personifications offered, a jealous friend or partner backstabbed this poor creature and lobed off its top! Very unlikely when it is people who corner the market on homicide. If a rodent had done the deed, why leave so much bird to waste? Waste is certainly a more human invention. And if it was a person, their tendencies would credit cruelty to the barbarian residing within some souls. Either way, it was a morose thing.

Poor Paris Pigeon. Done in and left to rot.

It got me thinking about all the other beings who carry our crumbs.

The living and dying of them.

Certainly they carry stories of their own as well.

Lost and unworthy as we may deem them.

Trustworthy as they were with our words and deeds wound tightly inside the shackles on their legs.

| 3 |

Paris Pigeon Sculpture 3rd arr.

Unmade

I am a breath I'll never take
A step toward the past
A moment in a future
I am nothing
And everything between
Your nothing and mine
Unmade at my beginning
A foregone conclusion
Realized in my prime
The song setting in a bird at dawn

My Solo

I'm not conversant with all the poets
education didn't serve me well
before I knew who I wanted to be

Only now with a wrinkled edge
can I trace Horace's hand painting
form and fiber into poetry
And exalt Sappho's lyrics
Only now can I discern the depths of Hell
See that Virgil illuminated Blake's way
Sense a fellow Gemini in Chaucer
I could often criticize and cry with Shakespeare
Yet only now
can I visualize the Gray mooring for Wheatley
Appreciate Emily's Capitol efforts
Walk above hell with Issa

Recently I walked with Baldwin
and Stein on Montparnasse
And in May believe I heard Langston's
blue suede shoes call out Ma'am

In June I finally felt Joy's lost land
as Maya held my hand.

Uncertified degrees of learning.
Paper, not always the best teacher
Time has taught me.
Grammar did not give the sonnet,
it gave it rails
I prefer to meander off course
Punctuation would ask the chorus
to sing abated
and deny free verse its aria
Absent notes complete the piece

My soul's song,
long quieted in the
buzz of busyness and
damper of disbelief,
must no longer go unsung
I'm an upswell, a kettle aboil
Do I trust the steep brew inside

I have tried to sing harmony
Now my dissonance must rise unfettered

Now I hear that faint trilling
Now my twilight solo pours forth
Filling voices within me unheard

52 Mondays

Time is a routine dream
Servant, the sun wakes a hard worker
or sends them to bed
but man needs a scapegoat to be on time.
The longest months are not the harshest.
For length isn't anything more than style.
A Viper or Boa both drape beautifully.
We are already closer to dead
at the long end of each.

A mullioned moon stretches its gaze
drowning us with light.
Dreaming beneath we slumber through life.

Numbered names prepackage our living
into busy colors and sometimes those boxes box us in.
Slow death too in 52 Mondays torturous
across seven day journeys.
A dozen chapters assuredly
will sell our seasons cheap in a printed copy next year.
Flipped as we are on photo filled pages

beginnings and endings sold
with pin up girls or cute canines help us through.
The final moment before a first is deemed last.
Who's winning?
Hours add up our scoreboard.
New moon passes intentions to a full.
Tests and failures outlive our efforts
And the tide still pulls at an age
Churning our water

Biting frost and stinging suns.
Heat and cold both soothe and burn
and a flower grows in each.

We can grow in harsh conditions you know
Becoming beautiful for it.
Despite bleak skies and our expiration
A month is it's own
and comes barreling at you or fleeting past
unless late in delivering our weather.
My lungs prefer an abiding chill to breathe.
Countless beauties and tragedies bloom
abundant in our chest.
Numbering the design of our days.

A Mind Swayed

Lost, a needle in my own haystack
I find myself in the pines
discarded among
slivers of copper laid at the feet of majesty,
shed only to begin again
towers of truth burn like matchsticks
My earth sticks a scent in nostrils
too filled with exhaust and falsehood
leading me home.
I run away.

Somewhere to be
Lights to switch on
Things to be busy with

My earth whispers stay and sway
in the ever decimated green
connected
rooted and reaching
Somewhere is here
see salvation in my light

Clamor only for the sky
Watch the moon widen and wane
Watch the moon watch us
devour ourselves in sticky gulps

Brave Relations

At first breath we are intrepid

A spinning dog chases the tail end of what's missing

Educate the home, pew and table
Raised to agree to enlist in a suitable fashion of servitude

Notions outside of rank sunk
Crushed carbon in the deep earth of ancestry

Diamonds discovered must shine
Looking for light they spar for viability within the den testing

Squashed into dirt unworthy
God watching as his judges determine humanity in their
omnipotence

Family first with a love conditioned
In agreement all is pardoned Silence overlooked at Sunday
supper

Voiced dissent targeted in venery

Prize mounted inclinations languish in a trophy room divided by Right

Seeking a win from a lost soul

Biased panel announces losers in a race to be heard and deemed Left

Permeable to frost we freeze

Words directed errantly at reason are unfound in Red faced defense

Finish line imagined uncrossed

Related to unrelatable set for dinner at torn places dressed unforgiving

Broken ties, aprons and dreams

Family tree severed for plucky pride finds no absolution in the roots

Constructed

Did I make a dent
My chiseled epitaph might ask

Heavy journals dusty with age
Might inquire vainly
If the earth felt my pull

Breath caught on morning's chill
Was it captured, exhausted
Evaporated, may I remain

Did expertly flipped eggs matter
To more than my few hungry loves
Was my soup filling

Credit scores won't answer
Calculations of my worth

Do I later languish in witty repose
Weighed in memory and deed
Google's remembrance card

Did time make good use of me
Was I left behind
Elsewhere, having done enough

Am I still holding on the eternal end
Documenting what cannot be defined
When even this mortgage can't lien on me

Can I sign myself into the book of life
Beyond the paltry census line

Will my tread have been too light
Dull dust blown from burnt bones
Unknown human fossil lies here

Did my force commune with good
Can my faith have been too expansive
Taxed in body and spirit, birth to grave

Did those stingy adjusters claim my value
When their fenders felt my impact
Living here has cost me dearly

I Could Just Not Care

This dream sticks in my crawl space
Eyelids painted in the broad strokes
of reality unseen
I'm there,
Where you go in dreams
Sun hidden in a haze
Over land no man can claim
The distance collapses into
A large tent, being erected
A kaleidoscope of cloth
Stitched by hands as vibrant
Draped by what we've made

Flaps flung wide, open in welcome

Earthen circle cradles weariness
Benched we sit side by side
Hands pressed in friendship
Leveled in faith, brushed with color
Ardent in ability, rooted in truth

Here to hear humanity trapped

In our unimaginable dance
Souls all, sing forgiveness
Notes strung on our banner
Ribbons, woven into my fabric
Harmonies hang in the balance
Mahatma and Langston spin center,
For Martin and Maya, June and Margaret,
Joy and James open up the floor
My dance card is full
Love invites in no hunger nor fear
Knowing those wolves can be held off
This dream contents me
Knowing those wolves can be held off

Two Candles

One flame devastates me
The sad quivering of cold fire
Tapered into the finest point of
loneliness
Is nearly too much to bear

When I am awful, a solitary flame
Lit to better deepen the darkness
can steal all oxygen from the room
can snuff all brilliance from my soul
can notify fighters of my internal fire

No amount of dousing dims
isolation
My spirit is a twin. Yin to life's Yang
I am both light and dark
And must burn for it

Shed

I was thinking
I needed to come out of my shell
and then I remembered that I'm just
getting started old as I am and as I've
crawled within and through myself
toward that lit end of promise that is today
I've gone nowhere but yesterday.

My start became my conclusion
How many acts does this play have?
Did denouement bypass the climax?

And why come out at all when this shell grows
with me weighted and lengthy, proud
of this tunnel I've burrowed, hollowed out, lived in,
Expanding only a fractal around my view
Sameness slapped over imbedded indifference
repairing old school walls with haphazard thought

And still age is tugging me toward tomorrow
like the drunk dragged face down onto bed

to try again in the morning to scuttle toward that
otherness lying beyond this filtered life
Visions lure the possible laid out before me
I hardly notice the smooth walls of my habit
Barely aware of the work forged against myself
A worm tilling her own soil

For how does one shed the shell of our own making
when wearing one's own garden planted by a mind
who feeds on the need for a shell.

The Way Away

The way across is unseen, unforged
 yet for a world of eyes and many billion feet.

For it must be our own eyes seeing to believe
our own feet fleeing to sense fear.

Our own way is at odds with ourselves
 for it does not tread over safe ground.

Preferring the swells of our hearts and minds,
Revisiting returns to ways once known,
We negotiate the detachment we allow.
The path is shared and squandered
Forcing us through and around the hurdles
We've laid in our way.

Leaving no trace or sign for our future selves
We eat the breadcrumbs.

Feeding the explorers waiting to rise among us
To conquer us then.

Favoured and feared
Four seasons cornered and squared
Scared
Conquered the dead while living
All Geminis need two faces
To see themselves in each other

What Has Beens

What has beens
Limiting ourselves by what has been

Origin opened our eyes, saw the end
Then charged us to live it

That which crept into Only
Grew from seeds meant for many
Born without thrones and tiaras
All deserve the distinction

Only, set hearts hard in gems
Void of prophecy
When stars sunk into soil
When iron banded us together weighted
When magnets pit cold poles between us
Seismic waves tossed our inertia
Rocked fascination to our surface
Inlaid our rivers with banks of gold, silver
Copper and maybes

Maybes became favorites
Greed envisioned favorites
Visions claimed power

Power forged belief
Belief built chains
Chains crush belief

Did our world ask us to build better selves
From stronger stuff, we, who suffer, base instincts
An eye for an eye has left us sightless
Lessons begotten forgotten
Atrocities willed by higher powers
Visions for our power
Ah, inventing spirit wield our swords
Through madmen praised and powerful
Blessings be our curse

What is the question that cannot be answered
How much can one add before it subtracts
Is there an equal answer
To the imbalance of our equation

Does one plus one only equal two
Maidens cannot carve into Mothers without Man

What carves deeper than the pools
Of wisdom set into the face of a Crone

Whitecaps

I've crossed under the white mainsail. Gliding across tumultuous water. Dark clouds move in. Behind. Always behind.

Sailcloth whips full. Bleached ripples wash over stories chased by truth. The depth of that storm. Outrun. Oncoming.

Carried by force, on fear. Unarmed labor pushes the prow that cuts into the heart of darkness.

Row. Row our boat.

Fell boards planed, joined by darker hands. Vessel carries all souls, forgets the blackest.

Murky water. Lost.

Decks swept clean in browned skin. Suns seen from other lands shine in scorched eyes.

Adrift, without room.

Rafts weigh on hopeful seas. Origins wash over borders drawn in pools of blood.

Power swells. Beats down.

Bounty in the hull. Crops watered by sweat, selfish seeds grown, that servitude plucked.

Mastered far afield.

Lanterns hung. Silence swaying on tolerance eaten in finger bowls tasted, tossed.

Light withheld.

Hymns held on the breeze, hummed on pink lips, rhythms natural, currents courageous.

Crushed on whitecaps.

Treasure sinks nameless in chains. Evaporating mist presses into heavy clouds to later rage.

Fathoms of tears.

We've crossed under the white mainsail. Stalling storms meant to reign down.

Upheaval. Tide turns.

Sail splits, furling into pages to read, lessons to conquer. Mast holds. A new charter.

Ahead. Always ahead.

We Can't Be Bothered With
The Flowers

Cracked homes for these shallow roots
Living in spite of confinement
Crowds in a crevice

Daring to dream without prettied protection
No walls around their gardens
Turning up unwanted thriving on neglect
Weeds

We can't be bothered with their flowers
Unblossomed slivers of defiance
Unfolding restricted arms
Wedged tightly into narrowness
So as to be unseen, unclean
To acknowledge underfoot makes them real
Planted

Tucked into crumbling outlines
Of concrete and stone barely nourished

Outstretched towards light
Newly paved slabs lie uninterrupted
But for fresh tufts of toughness
Wide rock rivers of progress crossed to find fertile soil
Pulled

Riches ripped from poor conditions
Nuisances noticed, tidy sacrifices
Dying dissenters rot

Grown for other starts to gain ground
Buried for better tended shoots
Cells tossed on beds to compost

Wright From Wrong

The sudden thunder
Startles the magnolias
To a deeper white
-Richard White haiku

Startled by the thunder
Did whiteness deepen the
Magnolia

Did a clamor for humanity
Ask too much shade
From a branch intoxicated
with its own stench

To smell the winds of change
In the charged air electric
Liberating

Sound from the crack
Of lightning's power

Stealing its own place
Back from a charged sky

Held quiet under switch
Do not all noses smell
Their own shiit

Pure perfume masks
All manner of pestilence
Does bloom know its rot
Whatever fruit may hang

Whipped into balms for believers
Blight spreads to the root
Nature's cure

Beaten by its own branch
March conquers darkness
Loud violence from within
Bursting forth in beauty

Your Dead Steps

Existing in your dead steps
Is the heave of your sigh
The weight of your burden
Hopelessness that rested under an obligated smile
Standing still in the defiance of your bearing

Dust remains unpaved under your departed treads
Miles forged were run over broken back and body
Imprints left for weaker feet to step in

Steering away from trails of scars your skin buried into our soil
Branched bodies press air from more treasured chests
Exhalations seen in your squashed and squandered seeds
Blood born in you beats in many hearts stopped and started
Pink with promise blackened by choice

Bones carried your story as far as they could
They till our soiled stories now

Silenced truths long rooted begin to grow
Fertile tears force us through this driving rain of blindness

Strung on the vapor we all take form from
Drenched in the sweat of your brow

Perpetual soles move us back and forth
Waves beating a rhythm then as now
Each, an exit that lingered

Scarred

I'd never carve a scar into a tree
But I see them carved
And wonder how a soul
Can purposefully do that
To another living thing

It's a judgment
I don't like to judge
Guilty.

Living among carvers
Having been carved
I simply wonder how.
The intention of it
The thing I can't get around

Certainly I've scraped
I know I've scratched
Never intended.

Never wanted to be the cause

Of war someone waged later
Most don't mean to maim
To feel better
Pain buries us under overtly

Slicing into another
Feeds our need
Question.

Collectively somewhere
Somehow later, if connected
Wired to a root system
Don't all feel wounds cut
Like this tree?

Or are we
Ripe or withering fruit
With long regret
Without apology?

Mapping scars on our land
On our hands at our hand
On our bodies in our minds
Topography deeply trenched
Stories and shame to share

Tougher skinned
Layers unfeeling
Between us.

Vagina Crossing

Procrastinating
in a world that bids us wait
for healthcare and humanity
makes us late
for modern times
for history's lesson
for tomorrow's plan
truth fled
as I waited for worse
and it came

When will tomorrow come
for today's people

Cocks will crow
logjams delay us all
men in muscle cars
pack the promenade
at this crossing

I cannot wait to cross

I must wait to cross
I cannot wade across
I shake off your cross
I must make it across
Cross me again

I've lingered

in my marginalized vagina this long
No rush to be recognized as whole
when controlled better broken

suck on this
bit chewed and spit out
a seed on the floor of your life
on that floor I'm kept

Swept under a system
a mind without body
a body without voice
a seed unplanted
More than seeds unplanted
No seed unplanted
sow your seeds
leave a wasteland to grow

We care to wait
wait to care
wait to carry

carry to wait
dull and lifeless
here cornered
digesting the bitter pill
gestating our enemies
birthing our fears
feeding our hopes
growing our saviors

She is the Shield She Wears

Morning world another night a beauty sleep a restless face washed to present

Best feet forward on shaky ground fracked and pocked with gunfire decor

The dawn of reality wakes her steaming cup in hand the news feeds her

Terror over toast

Dressed to succeed tailored in heels prancing pony jumping for a ribbon

Cubed and pressed down under the window she looks through looked at

Quips about how great her ass looks in those pants that skirt this light

Sits her ass down

Torn between the attention she's been taught to crave and a gnawing sense

Of wrong ways sideways glances and cornered elevators never going up boxed in

The room in the office in the bed in the country that folds into a world she hardly knows
Outside of the end

Coming served with equal sides of fear and hate fires and grim souls burning for dessert
Turns away from endangered species such as herself needing protection climbing a tree out
Of the fray walking running in sleep toward dreams always wakened by the nightmare
Keeping her stabled

Flying on fairytale wishes saving herself and the dragons from knights in the towers
Picturing her princess portrait in baggy sweats hair in a tie with love that looks her in the eye
Knowing the fairytale is waking herself with the kiss she'd give away to others just before she Steps over the abyss

Redressing Women

Pretend play with a name
Left at the foot of little girls' beds
Palimpsests with a past

Forced from home discarded in His favor
Hopeful chests filled innocence lost
Trophies taken in beds and haylofts
Promoting heirs and affairs

Words stifled thoughts silenced
Polite voices Cause no commotion
Kept quiet in corsets and corners
Play things placed at elbows dangled and dropped

Good bedfellows lie still
Legacy and land once Hers to walk
Given to good Sir for safekeeping
Stewards of nothing

All work and no play
Owned without ownership

Readied in rich lined pockets
A child berth carved out

For pleasure and produce
Burdens carried in womb
Hearts and arms weighed
Prepared to pass power to mister to man

Daughters appraised
Florences fighting and dying
Unmarked graves cross all borders
There are no reparations for women

No treaties signed no protocols
No declared end of conflict for

War crimes on women

Mothers reclaim a right
Not to marry without land or title returned

No theft compensated to generations
Halved to feed hunger's child
Broken to keep full
the cup in man's hand

Female selves embedded
Heirlooms pawned now
Valued higher non negotiable

Women's Hood

Smileless faces and deadpan eyes
Kodak captured the veils worn after a wedding
Sepia stole the red from a rose
The blush in a cheek
Monochrome missed the chocolate river or blue bird
Flying through an iris from anywhere
Stony statues of women haunt us in grey tone
Flimsy reminders of lives lived
Nameless women next to their men, birthing
Generations, iterations, variations
Hiding in the bared foot, the heeled shoe, the muddy hem
Textures stripped from our sisters' days

Unseen, are the rough worn or under utilized hands
The dreams tucked into aprons
Secrets burned in a well tended fire
How brilliant and burdened
Were those thoughts without voice or venue
What did they wish upon stars
What streaks of genius have we missed in our skies

Hidden in the animal skin and woolen smock
The sackcloth or silk frock
What ideas were lost above a lacey neckline
Beneath ringlets, waves and hat pins

Garments, the false guards against our weather
The dirty laundry tirelessly cleaned
The crush of thoughtfully crocheted pillows
under mans' boot

Womanhood runs longer than bolts of fabric
Its threads stand stronger
Against men, beneath parents
Before children, between each other

While some squeezed breaths into corsets
Others hid in trousers and marriage
Shallowly we are painted into yesterday's pages
Pretty and petty, given a tea cup to experience the ocean

How many now lost dared to achieve
What choices were achieved only to be lost
Put your ear up to mans' mouth to hear the answer

Without Freedom we remain
Having born our advocates or oppressors
We find ourselves in full color now
The future will know our filtered smiles
Will see our shades and strands

Will know we've chosen to be
Somewhere between painted and petty
and Taken seriously

Our creative hands now receive credit
They can alter the brightness
With which we are seen
Earning, winning, organizing, leading
Still asking permission to own our body
Wistfully we await our wombs

Hope is a fabric long spun of women
Knit with protest, planning, power and pain
Woven en masse may we one day lay our cloth
At an elected table

Make your choice don't make mine
Your laws have not governed my safety
Your laws only add to your untended flock

Our daughters cannot be reduced to what was
Strapped in a bra, surname or style
that describes who you want us to be.

So poured into a mini skirt or pant suit
Our armor dresses us for the coming war
With nips free or tightly bound
Our daily face paint readies us for battle

With ourselves until all women believe
We have earned a place at that table

Fort Womb

Whose side are you on? Procreation or its con

Battles waged in staunch men's rooms

Here they march upon Fort Womb

Wrapped in god and wrapped in gold

Bought for property, sold for control

Mercenary, missionary, grifter, thief

Rapist weak to want and greed

Ripe young fruit, a women plucked

Things to be hoed, plowed and fucked

Spoils of war, artillery claimed

No matter the mother or uterus maimed

Bent to broken tending to harvest

Who can push a body farthest

Wombs hold dirty secret and deed,

Keeper of sweet and unsavory seed

Good soil tilled ready for slaughter,

Pontification, command and fodder

Goddess, Mother, Maiden, Crone

Never too young and never too old

Carry our future, carry our shame

Carry to term or you'll be to blame

Mothers can dream and men can gloat

Guv'nors can scheme cause children will vote

Numbers added to a band

Brothers' guns in every hand

Bear our arms and bear our army

Only man should kill your baby

Drafted, neglected, payments unmade

Mother's tears the sacrifice paid

Power, land and pussy to grab

Battlements seized and daughters had

Fight the man, then bear the babe

Legacy passed our souls be saved

Starve it, bully it, beat and abhor it

Love it, adopt it but don't dare abort it

Carry our future carry our shame

Carry to term or you'll be to blame

Under banner of moral and greed

All of you women must cower and breed

Be our oxygen, tinder and fuel

Live out life by our ancient rule

Signs of the devil penned in Texas

Cover your sins and cover your asses

Rape and pillage and plunder reward

Stick them with love, blood or the sword

Men will strut and judge and flee

Then collect ten thousand in fees

Women will push and burn and scream

And lose the right to the right to deem

Bounty in uterus, fetus and womb

Woman has always held man's tomb

Still

I hear the loudness
of this quiet
Utterly silent
but for the leaves
Traipsing over each other
how alone it feels
Not to be heard
on the breeze
I am still listening
many I bring along
Take no space
to occupy my thoughts
And I like to be here
my self and no other
Invaded by noises unmade

Small

To safeguard small
Close doors on the stranger

Savor what is known, spit out the bits
that really need a chew

There is peace found in a path well worn,
tread beneath your feet owned

Akin to time on copper, rubbed for luck
small circles won't surprise

Comfort is found slipping into boots
still stuck with yesterday's mud

Sink into the same pebble in a shoe,
brush a hand on the same rough tree at the bend

See the vista halfway through, the one that could
send a mind reeling, soaring, exploring, knowing

Reel it in.
Too wide a range is a world with other places to be

What else is needed but this view
to those who learned to read by this light

Better the hole in this sock,
reliably there this morning as it was last night

Can't imagine those other holes,
how comforting they might feel on other feet.

In the Stew

We didn't hear the words then
That we hear
Now

Those sounds got lost in the soup served up on
Sundays and slopped onto individual trays
Held in school lunch lines

Standing behind
Others

Beings who sucked other bits
From the stew of their knowing
Pieces we could not swallow
In places we never stood
Still we walk that time together

Waiting in lines promising to bring us
Closer
Hearing the same dinner bells
Calling on us to show up

To remember we are
Expected

Asking us to raise our hand when answers are in
Short supply
We are elemental at our shared table
Dug into the earth deep with hunger
Feeding on the resources
we peeled and cut and gathered from
Ourselves

Time Has Spent Us

Walking circles in stopwatch suits
Time has spent us

Pinned with always and nevers on lapels
Tightly stitched together
Bursting at the seams
Hemmed in by ourselves

God, I'm sick of demigods

Building worlds within this world for themselves
Blocking median dignity and a livable wage
Extincting average man from his right to exist

Global crises denied from this, hot, tub
Sinking. Polar bears tread our waters
Billions float on faith,
Aren't we supposed to deny false idols?
Pundits, our parodies, shirk humanity with ignorance

Headline! Self importance is our greatest failure
TV news runs misdiagnosed in the background

If we are in God's image does she wear glasses?
Jesus didn't ask us
To pull ourselves up by our sandal straps

Who are our demons if not ourselves?
Who can we blame if God does not exist?
We are the monsters under our bed

Buddha asks us
To suffer the suffering of one another

Truest angels and devils
Rest in the set of our shoulders
Hardened marshmallows all

Meeting onces and seconds with a million excuses
Waiting to live out truths, hidden
Writ large, amicus curiae, judge and jury

Creative in our constructions and destructions
Drawing lines to separate sinew and skin, dogma and kin
Crate trained for pissing matches

I'm boxed in

Encased into confines shackled to the show
If it's not barreling down the shaft of a gun
If it's not squaring us off into corners

Can we trust it?

If we didn't start the fire,
Who is fanning these flames?

Tomorrows are in high demand
And my patience is in short supply

This world is wasting away, better visit soon
Terra firma, marina or tarmac
No place holds Safe

We've declared war on such things
As love.

If it's not streaming into our homes
If it's not what we want to believe

Can we believe it?

Science, religion or data
No place holds Truth

We've demanded stupid is
As does

Blazing, sinking, melting,
Dying to fly from these places
Built for ourselves, from ourselves.

God, I'm sicker still for my children
Living with a hard stop
Our alarms blaring we press snooze

*amicus curiae= Latin. Translated' friend of the court'.

Blurry Windows

I feel the living leaving my step
Creaks of my own doors, shutting out possibility
Watching the world through blurry windows,
Tears leak
Into a rotting frame
Seeing fewer surprises in the breakage
Perhaps we must cry to see through the pains

When a smaller self saw age it was with wonder
For all that was known,
Seen and secreted.
Hidden Ingredients in a family recipe
Youth rarely sees the stores
Of wasted wealth living inside a million wishes to grow up.

Legs that climbed ladders mine couldn't
Left me in the dust
Until I could return the favor.
That circle comes round

Beauty lives in the rips and wrinkles of a lifetime etched

Deeply lined faces, and careening valleys of minds,
The maps, we all get lost in

This traveler has further to go
On less steam
Still these feet can step
And onward they will go

Though upkeep on this house is in shambles.
Shudders shame me in the chill breeze
Springs are growing shorter.

Graveyard

The sea, that graveyard for dreams,
    and dwelling of deeper life
Roars in our ears, the swells, the crests of our hearts.
We live. We fight to stay alive. We die.
Greater visions have swayed us beneath sylvan mast
    cut or carved we aren't saved.
Those yellowing fields follow us home, seasoned.
A radiant sun rises and sets on our seconds.
Linked, bound, distinctive cells in a body
    attempting to straighten a circle.
Antagonists in our own stories, chained
For only when each link welcomes the bird to alight
Ardent in action to further its soar,
    only then will the world know peace.

The World Yet

Nothing has happened in the world yet

Sleep still corners my eyes
Dawn has dawned and I wake warm

War isn't on my pillow
Fear isn't in my head

First awareness sees light only as
Winks of wonder adjust the darkness of dreams

This ignorance may be my only bliss

Testimony

This heart remembers a sun filled day when filtered through child's eyes the tangle of artfully veined leaves, both brilliant and black looked down. An erected web of trunk and branch stretched above, anchored underfoot the muddy earth stood warm and steady.

Youth and innocence had yet to be conquered, I'd not lived a decade. In that moment,

surmounted by the awe of uncertainty, intuitively I became aware that I was not meant to understand all. Possessed by tremendous beauty, the balance of light and shadow held me dizzy beneath its power.

Witness to the connectedness of life.

One certainty took root and has held.

We are part of something deep and meaningful.

The world would surely balance that particular sun filled day with storms soon enough. Silvered leaves would turn against the furious skies cycling round me, my bent branches, broken. Peace would come later in understanding one could not be without the other. The sun and the storm.

Appreciate the balance. We cannot struggle in vain and cannot vainly struggle.

Peace is larger than a sign, larger than peacetime, larger than the end of a war.

While worlds rage, peace is revealed in each moment of grace, dignity and empathy.

My work must reflect what must be lost to be gained, what must be unknown to feel assured, what equal truths lie at our feet and in our hearts.

Writing is seeking truth, discovering worth, clinging waves, surrendering to night's magic, dawning from within deep valleys, climbing nearly imperceptible ladders of hope, rising against the drag of gravity's pull and our broken hearts.

Ripple

Ring your truth in a skipped stone a wish plunked
Into watery troughs of possible
Indentations of what makes you *you*
Dipped into space and time, a theory of us
Impressions left on skin in a heart on a mind
A star sunken into elsewhere unseen
A course charted below the surface

Points join above land skimming our seas
An ache stretching stratosphere for connection
Stones in a pond, stars in someone's sky
Pulsating points of light pinned in word and deed
Constellations strung out on what is known
Standing next to truth weighed and uncounted next to you
Look a brushed shoulder in the eye to realize more

Toxic or tonic we infect sensibility
Each of us a Geiger counter being counted
Contagious with energy we radiate outward
Absorbed by osmosis and symbiosis and all the osis

Synthesized synergized terrorized harmonized
Before we become outlines
Silt displaced doesn't disappear into the firmament

I Am In That Stroke

I am in that stroke
Of the painter who left marks on the archaeology of us
Shown wide then tapered like the passion of new love
See me in the pressure mounting and fading
I'm in the corner just there sidelined but necessary
A hint a signal of who I was intended to be
Known, traced thinly on thick paper
A dull impression not quite erased
A blot of brilliance dabbed then smeared onto a palette
I am the brilliant storm on Jupiter
In this speck collected and mounted
Largeness captured clinging to cosmos made small
I am seen in the artwork of us hung to be revealed
My eyes tell me I was in the thought that conceived it
If not as muse then as spectator I was considered
Pinned to a place in our time

True Grime

City grit
Indubitably absolute
Tried, tested beneath feet
Tarred, broken under treaded rubber
Filthy tribulations laid bare
Elements returning to rest
Function exposed
Wadded and wasting in cornered crevice

Human rift
Scent of heinous inaction
Expelled effort and loss
Decaying breath escapes through gasp and wisp
Siloed fractals on sidewalks
Isolated salt grains in a tin
Bumping ignorant
Tear stained torn and wanting angry in silence

Detritus dropped
An anthropology of now
Wafted bits strewn once whole

Lost on the tide of necessity and access
Cognizance soaked in neglect
Unused good and extras elected
Avoidable death
Crusted coffin weighs down on her core

Bequest made
Reading the will as its written
Watermarks blazened unique
Each heedless step presses a decision indicted
Insolent singulars esteemed by their mirrors
The sum is less than a part
Character corroded
Hoggish pinpoints map a demise

Wanton Sucklings

SPLIT open we spill onto her immaculate floor
Spoiled seeds of a mother walk heedless
Headlong
Headstrong
Away from her concern
Testing boundaries at home
Tormenting her guests
Unearthing abundance in lieu of treasure

There's no place like home yet we
Bury what is for what may yet be

Carelessly we carve into our heritage

Stealing the matches scorching her curtains
Aflame with our desire
Her face bears the scars of our
Willful spats

Mother roars at our stupidity with a tsunami

A wave of reason on our shores
A soothing breeze on our faces hot with hatred

She loves us even when we don't get along
Flawed offspring compensated with gifts we squander
At our feet she lays moonshine, and treeshade,
colors beyond imagining
the tinkling bells of a stream, the screech of an owl

We will not sit still and listen

Maybe if we didn't sell our soils and souls
For figments, for fissures, for the
Imaginary paper and flags we carry
Without tribute our arrogance flies
Rippling on a wind we don't own and still harness
Our ribbons flap in the face of our birthright

Mother winces at the slight

She caves to our demands caters to foolish whims
And places golden delights in our hands
Still we rifle her wardrobe for precious gems

Little control over her unruly flock
Left wanting for sorrys that will come too late

Too late to fill voids we have left in our potential
Her tears sting our cheeks as they rain from her

Skies ignored unless they weather us well
She distracts with the glint of metal lodged in her chest
We stab her heart for metal to lodge in chests

Ignorance is bliss we are told
What will she do with these ungrateful children
Wanting ever more than we are given

We push riches into closets to make room for our greed
Stealing from our siblings we spoil our home
Wanton sucklings are we
Nursing ourselves to death
This messy brood

A haggard Mother bathes us in her pools
Laundering our filth
Drying out her tears

Spring Before Winter

Spring is here before winter had her chance
May flowers won't wait for showers raining north for Imbolc
Mittens kept waiting in pockets we warm our days

As active Man swims through glacier canyons
Rivers of warmth carve into old ice dying young
Titanic structures melt wreckage into a rising sea

Losing ground White hunters adapt to endangerment
With mans crushing hand stretching four corners
A planet gasps as our lungs disappear

Resources shrink wrap progress
With heartbeats withering in flashes of flood in hell's fire
We absolve unique beats dying for our furniture

Unnatural dark wizards are we -conjuring chemical living
Ease our burden with strawberries in winter
Life is chosen only for some as we sell short for power

Flick a switch to turn off minds -package up dim hearts

Humans don't own an earth we lay claim to
Running rivers of steel through highways of life

Perversions of manscape reverse reasoned season
As grimly reaped rubber reefs create skeletons
Our view is spectacular for the end of the world

No foresight in foreskins raping Earth
Honor is lost in each meter of soil turned
We kneecap a cheetah so we can run

Gyre

My feet are cold
Circulation isn't circling back into the warmth of my heart
maybe my heart isn't as warm as it once was
from eating sugars made cheap for the impoverished
or pricey for specialty seekers
      as we heat and chill
      cold always follows heat
maybe my feet feel as frigid as death from saving the energy bill
or from unwashed socks
or watching the coldness that has overcome my fellows
my kindred my unknown enemies
the switch we flip to turn off humans
powered by the currents running hot and cold

Maybe when heat leaves it goes elsewhere

Could it be the Ocean heating keeps my feet cold
or that we share similar concern
with plastic bags meant to carry our load easier
as she wonders why in her Menopause
      without pause

    she churns our chum
gyres circulating the stories of our priorities
unnourished children living in a garbage pouch
sea life marsupials sucking on synthetic teets
tied to the beach with our six ringed pack
beer pong seems so easy before its beached
My feet in the warming water are still cold

Maybe easy doesn't go elsewhere

Parched

Dry the chalky river
Where we made our bed

Parched souls now wane
When a wise world went unheeded

Unphased moons waxed
In a waiting sky silky with indifference

We paint ourselves thickly
Earth clogs with our selfish reminder

Heavy in our stroke we hang
Portraits the earth won't want to remember

Decomposing Sunflowers

The Sunflower is the national flower of Ukraine

Spring solstice came and went
Still the chill clings to shattered glass
And a sugar moon watches on
As bombs land in living rooms
As roadways became lifelines
As fire rains down on schools

Art and people go underground

A playground swing creaks
The baker does what he can
Amid the rubble flowers grow
The yield wasted
the dead fertilizing our fields

On we walk to fight or flee
Past mass graves
As is the way

A new sunflower head
Reaches toward the sun
And stands witness to our nature

Sunflower Shadows

senryū

The world has broken my focus
My comfortable stare is uncomfortable
And I cannot look away

Haiku

Words left unsaid sift
       through silence a kettle boils
on summer pavement

Centered

Where I am is lit
By the truths I have not told
Darkened by the lies
Shared so easy over supper
Seen by none other
Than my minds eye

All of it seems
Inconsequential
In the living of it
Dwelling somewhere
Between Earth's center
And the moon

Miracle

Goes by in a blink
Doesn't it?
Or 40 winks
Or 51 years or 1.6 million seconds
or an eon
Or whatever other form of measurement
We humans invented

Inescapable the belief in a timed reality
A hand goes round
Guiding this tour of Earth

Though it is entirely possible
We may have been timeless before
We number our days now

I've lived and am living
Breaths. I take them
And leave them in yesteryear
along with my easy bake holly hobbie oven
and my innocence

and Mother only knows what else.

And who's giving them?
These breaths
Queries the sage raging eternal at the age old question
For if I'm taking them they must have been given
I'd like to thank the academy and my parents

For this gift so freely given that payments
are extracted by the loan shark of existence
Nothing costs us everything.

And yet they come, repeatedly, effortlessly
breaths so impossible to ignore they must be mine

Like clamoring children at my heels claiming me theirs
and don't I bring them both into being by noticing them?
Choosing to convey them through the ins and outs of me?

I keep Breathing. I must want to or I wouldn't
Wouldn't I
Breathing
Life enters me,
Organic groves swell with purpose
Filling, quickening, ripening, spoiling
The fruit of me exits these mechanical cavities
Life leaves me
Life enters
Life leaves

Over and over and Ever since we were pink and newborn.
And now still,
Though I'm farther from new.

Breathe.
The very word returns us to something so instinctive
we've forgotten to credit ourselves for the doing of it
Many who did now don't

Seeking and releasing this air
returns my life to the balance of all things.
For if it has been here so must it be gone
and tomorrow was always a dream.

Childhood passed in breaths
I didn't count until it counted and now they don't add up
Subtracting as they do
Precious thing this living

Youth has swirled and swung round
like the water stuck to the bottom of a bucket,
fast and miraculous the inertia of it all,
with aging waiting

in the mirror of the puddle forming beneath the pail
Muddied

Winded I spin in the mess of this living,
for once I wore diapers

now incontinence sends me ads
and isn't the ring of life's cycle
so clear
that ring so clear
That ring going round ringing-
ringing as it goes round and round
as I go round and ring out
as that bucket lists,
spins and spills into tomorrow
and you know what, I'm along for that ride.

Indebted to the many great wordsmiths, who, across time, have poured into my mind, that fortunate sieve, their thought-filled prose and poetry, landing with meteoric impact, creating expansive craters, proliferating new shoots in this inner earth child turned late bloomer.

I recognize the many voices left out of the discussion and will lash the weight of unheard work to mine with intentional sapience, vigilance and deviant authority.

Sincerest thanks to my dearest love, Damon, and our two verdant offshoots, Nillin and Deej, for often agreeing to listen to just one more poem.... Lori, for the words you've pinned to your walls. Mom, family and friends are a fortune with which I am indeed wealthy, sincere thanks all.

For intentional community, time and space to share, thank you to staff and members of The Mercantile Library and to the Ohio Poetry Association for tireless officers and energetic appointees. Love & Light to all my fellow poets, writers, regular readers and listeners. I value the leadership and energy around poetry, especially that of Chuck Salmons and Christopher Minton of the Ohio Poetry Association, Norman Finkelstein, Patti Niehoff, Manuel Iris the Poet Laureate of the City of Cincinnati from 2018-2020, John Burroughs the 2022-2023 U.S. National Beat Poet Laureate, Jonie McIntire the Poet Laureate of Lucas County in Toledo, Yalie Saweda Kamara, Ph.D., the Poet Laureate of Cincinnati 2022-2024

-HBR